# WHAT
# *Daughters*
## TEACH US

# WHAT
# *Daughters*
# TEACH US

*Life's Lessons Learned From Our Girls*

Willow Creek Press

Published by Willow Creek Press
P.O. Box 147, Minocqua, Wisconsin 54548

Editor: Andrea Donner

**Photo Credits**

© **Peter Arnold, Inc.**: p.10 © Claudia Schiffner/Bilderberg; p.57 © Susanna Rescio/Bilderberg;
p.61 © Angelika Jakob/Bilderberg; p.70 © David Cavagnaro; p.73 © Bill O'Connor;
p.78 © Helga Lade; p.90 © Eberhard Grames

© **Norvia Behling**: p.18; p.62 © Daniel Johnson

© **Corbis**: page 33 © Hannah Mentz/zefa/Corbis

© **Dusty Rose Kenney / www.thedustyimage.com**: pages 2, 6, 9, 14, 21, 22, 29

© **Barbara Peacock / www.barbarapeacock.com**: pages 26, 38, 41, 50, 53, 54, 58, 65, 74, 89

© **Superstock.com**: p.13 © Ron Dahlquist; p.17 © Hill Creek Pictures;
p.25 © The Copyright Group; p.30 © age fotostock; p.34 © Tom Rosenthal;
p.37 © age fotostock; p.45 © Mauritius; p.46 © age fotostock; p.49 © age fotostock;
p.66 © age fotostock; p.77 © age fotostock; p.81 © Hill Creek Pictures;
p.85 © age fotostock; p.86 © age fotostock; p.93 © Hill Creek Pictures; p.94 © age fotostock

Printed in Canada

*While we try to teach our children all about life,*
*Our children teach us what life is all about.*

Angela Schwindt

*Babies are such a nice way to start people.*

Don Herold

# a m a z e m e n t

*What greater thing is there for human souls than
to feel that they are joined for life—to be with each other
in silent unspeakable memories.*

George Eliot

*You can't plan the kind of deep love that results from having children.*

Unknown

# a w e

*A babe in the house is a well-spring of pleasure,*
*a messenger of peace and love, a resting place for innocence*
*on earth, a link between angels and men.*

Martin Fraquhar Tupper

*The only thing worth stealing is a kiss from a sleeping child.*

Joe Houldsworth

# blessedness

*Children make you want to start life over.*

Muhammad Ali

*In America there are two classes of travel—*
*first class, and with children.*

Robert Benchley

# challenges

*Even when freshly washed and relieved of all obvious confections,*
*children tend to be sticky.*

Fran Lebowitz

*It is not easy to be crafty and winsome at the same time,*
*and few accomplish it after the age of six.*

John W. Gardner and Francesca Gardner Reese

# c h a r m

*Let us be grateful to people who make us happy, they are*
*the charming gardeners who make our souls blossom.*

Marcel Proust

*Children find everything in nothing.*

Giacomo Leopardi

# creativity

*Every child is an artist.*

Pablo Picasso

*A child can ask questions that a wise man cannot answer.*

Unknown

# curiosity

*Childhood is measured out by sounds and smells and sights,*
*before the dark hour of reason grows.*

John Betjeman

A little girl is sugar and spice and everything nice—
especially when she's taking a nap.

Unknown

# defiance

If you have never been hated by your child
you have never been a parent.

Bette Davis

*Childhood is the most beautiful of all life's seasons.*

Unknown

# e n c h a n t m e n t

*The greatest poem ever known
Is one all poets have outgrown:
The poetry, innate, untold,
Of being only four years old.*

Christopher Morley

*The hardest part of raising a child is teaching them to ride bicycles.*
*A shaky child on a bicycle for the first time needs both support and freedom.*
*The realization that this is what the child will always need can hit hard.*

Sloan Wilson

# encouragement

*The central struggle of parenthood is to let our*
*hopes for our children outweigh our fears.*

Ellen Goodman

*Youth is a perpetual intoxication; it is a fever of the mind.*

Francois Duc de la Rochefoucauld

# energy

*What is a home without children? Quiet.*

Henny Youngman

*You have to ask children and birds how cherries and strawberries taste.*

Johann Wolfgang von Goethe

# e n j o y m e n t

*Sweet childish days, that were as long*
*As twenty days are now.*

William Wordsworth

*No day can be so sacred but that the laugh of a*
*little child will make it holier still.*

Robert Green Ingersoll

# exuberance

*Where children are, there is the golden age.*

Novalis

A daughter is a little girl who will grow up to be a friend.

Unknown

# friendship

We may find some of our best friends in our own blood.

Ralph Waldo Emerson

*Kids: they dance before they learn there is anything that isn't music.*

William Stafford

# f u n

*Only where children gather is there any real chance of fun.*

Mignon McLaughlin

*What feeling is so nice as a child's hand in yours?*
*So small, so soft and warm, like a kitten huddling*
*in the shelter of your clasp.*

Marjorie Holmes

# g e n t l e n e s s

*A child's hand in yours—what tenderness it arouses,*
*what power it conjures. You are instantly*
*the very touchstone of wisdom and strength.*

Marjorie Holmes

*A laugh is a smile that bursts.*

Mary H. Waldrip

# giggles

*You can't deny laughter; when it comes, it plops down
in your favorite chair and stays as long as it wants.*

Stephen King

*A daughter is a day brightener and a heart warmer.*

Unknown

# goodness

*Every child born has innate goodness.*

Chinese proverb

*A child is a curly dimpled lunatic.*

Ralph Waldo Emerson

# goofiness

*Insanity is hereditary;*
*you get it from your children.*

Ralph Waldo Emerson

*There is a garden in every childhood, an enchanted place*
*where colors are brighter, the air softer,*
*and the morning more fragrant than ever again.*

Elizabeth Lawrence

# h a p p i n e s s

*Think what a better world it would be if we all, the whole world,*
*had cookies and milk about three o'clock every afternoon*
*and then lay down on our blankets for a nap.*

Barbara Jordan

*What the daughter does, the mother did.*

Jewish proverb

# heritage

*And thou shalt in thy daughter see,*
*This picture, once, resembled thee.*

Ambrose Philips

*Children are a wonderful gift... They have an extraordinary
capacity to see into the heart of things
and to expose sham and humbug for what they are.*

Desmond Tutu

# honesty

*Pretty much all the honest truth-telling
there is in the world is done by children.*

Oliver Wendell Holmes

*Every child begins the world again...*

Henry David Thoreau

# h o p e f u l n e s s

*Every child comes with the message that God
is not yet discouraged of man.*

Rabindranath Tagore

*One of the virtues of being very young is that you don't let the facts get in the way of your imagination.*

Sam Levenson

# i m a g i n a t i o n

*There are no seven wonders of the world in the eyes of a child. There are seven million.*

Walt Streightiff

*A child's world is fresh and new and beautiful,*
*full of wonder and excitement.*

Rachel Carson

# innocence

*Maybe that is why young people make success.*
*They don't know enough.*

Richard P. Feynman

*The older I get, the more I marvel at the wisdom of children.*

David Morgan

# intelligence

*Children are remarkable for their intelligence and ardor,*
*for their curiosity, their intolerance of shames,*
*the clarity and ruthlessness of their vision.*

Aldous Huxley

*Anyone who thinks the art of conversation is dead*
*ought to tell a child to go to bed.*

Robert Galagher

# inventiveness

*Children are like wet cement.*
*Whatever falls on them makes an impression.*

Dr. Haim Ginott

*The young and the old are closest to life.*
*They love every minute dearly.*

Chief Dan George

# j o y

*Children have neither past nor future;*
*they enjoy the present, which very few of us do.*

Jean de la Bruyere

No one has yet realized the wealth of sympathy, the kindness
and generosity hidden in the soul of a child.

Emma Goldman

# kindness

Children remind us to treasure the smallest gifts,
even in the most difficult of times.

Allen Klein

*I am thankful for laughter,*
*except when milk comes out of my nose.*

Woody Allen

# laughter

*At the height of laughter, the universe is*
*flung into a kaleidoscope of new possibilities.*

Jean Houston

*A daughter is a gift of love.*

Unknown

# l o v e

*There's something like a line of gold thread running through a man's words when he talks to his daughter, and gradually over the years it gets to be long enough for you to pick up in your hands and weave into a cloth that feels like love itself.*

John Gregory Brown

*Children are a great comfort in your old age—*
*and they help you reach it faster too.*

Lionel Kauffman

# m i s c h i e f

*A child is a most desirable pest.*

Max Gramlich

*A daughter may outgrow your lap,*
*but she will never outgrow your heart.*

Unknown

# preciousness

*Children are the bridge to heaven.*

Persian proverb

*A daughter is the happy memories of the past,*
*the joyful moments of the present,*
*and the hope and promise of the future.*

Unknown

# promise

*There is always one moment in childhood*
*when the door opens and lets the future in.*

Graham Greene

Many a man wishes he were strong enough
to tear a telephone book in half—
especially if he has a teenage daughter.

Guy Lombardo

# rebelliousness

Any astronomer can predict with absolute accuracy just where
every star in the universe will be at 11:30 tonight. He can make
no such prediction about his teenage daughter.

James T. Adams

*If you look in the eyes of the young, you see flame.*

Victor Hugo

# restlessness

*Teenagers complain there's nothing to do,*
*then stay out all night doing it.*

Bob Phillips

*Of all the haunting moments of motherhood,*
*few rank with hearing your own words*
*come out of your daughter's mouth.*

Victoria Secunda

# sassiness

*Ask the young. They know everything.*

Joseph Joubert

*Watching your daughter being collected
by her date feels like handing over
a million dollar Stradivarius to a gorilla.*

Jim Bishop

# self-reliance

*We've had bad luck with our kids—
they've all grown up.*

Christopher Morley

*You don't have to suffer to be a poet.*
*Adolescence is enough suffering for anyone.*

John Ciardi

# s e n s i t i v i t y

*At fourteen you don't need sickness or death for tragedy.*

Jessamyn West

*It's lovely to be silly at the right moment.*

Horace

# silliness

*A characteristic of the normal child is
she doesn't act that way very often.*

Unknown

*Mother Nature is providential. She gives us twelve years to develop*
*a love for our children before turning them into teenagers.*

William Galvin

# s l o p p i n e s s

*The invention of the teenager was a mistake. Once you identify*
*a period of life in which people get to stay out late*
*but don't have to pay taxes—*
*naturally, no one wants to live any other way.*

Judith Martin

As a teenager you are at the last stage in your life when
you will be happy to hear that the phone is for you.

Fran Lebowitz

# sociability

If your children spend most of their time in
other people's houses, you're lucky;
if they all congregate at your house, you're blessed.

Mignon McLaughlin

*Children in a family are like flowers in a bouquet:*
*there's always one determined to face in an opposite direction*
*from the way the arranger desires.*

Marcelene Cox

# stubbornness

*You have to hang in there, because two or three years later, the*
*gremlins will return your child, and she will be wonderful again.*

Jill Eikenberry

The finest qualities of our nature, like bloom on fruits,
can be preserved only by the most delicate handling.

Henry David Thoreau

# tenderness

Always kiss your children goodnight—
even if they're already asleep.

H. Jackson Brown, Jr.

*Love is just a word until someone comes along and gives it meaning.*

Unknown

# unconditional
# love

*Children are love made visible.*

American proverb